CONTENTS

Fit for life

What is your life? It's the time you have to spend enjoying yourself, exploring the world and achieving whatever you want to achieve. And since there's so much to see, do and discover, most people hope to live for as long as they can.

In the wealthier countries of the world, most teenagers today can expect to live for around 80 years.

Make the most of it!

To make the most of your life, it helps to be healthy and active for as much of it as possible. That way, you can keep doing whatever you want, and enjoying the life you have.

Maybe you love tennis now...

You'll be into dance when you're older...

You might take up yoga one day...

And run a marathon when you're retired!

Ways to be healthy

Keeping fit is about keeping your body working well, and avoiding illnesses and injuries. Taking exercise is one of the most important ways you can do this, and that's mainly what this book is about.

But exercise doesn't just work on its own. There are loads of ways you can look after your body, from eating well to getting enough sleep, and they all work together.

Where are you on the well-being scale?

RUN DOWN

DOING OK

NOT VERY WELL

ZINGGG!

All of these aspects of health and fitness play a part in keeping you happy and well.

Eating and drinking
Food keeps you alive, and gives you the fuel your body needs to keep moving.

Exercise
Moving around keeps your body in shape and ready for action.

Mental health
The health of your mind, meaning moods, emotions and dealing with stress, is closely related to exercise.

Avoiding illness
Know how to dodge germs and spot symptoms, and see diseases off.

Sleep
You need sleep to keep your body and brain working. You can't live without it!

Look after yourself
It's important to keep yourself clean and care for your body.

Of course, it's not possible to do all of these things 100 per cent right, 100 per cent of the time but they all help towards keeping you healthy and happy.

What actually happens inside your body when you move around and exercise? Take a look...

Muscles and bones

Your body can move the way it does thanks to your muscles and bones – also called your musculoskeletal system (right).

So what makes you move? Imagine you see a ball and want to kick it. First, your eyes send a signal to your brain. Your brain thinks and makes a decision, then swings into action.

Your skeleton is made up of over 200 bones.

Muscles surround your bones and attach to them in lots of different places.

Muscles are fixed onto bones by strong, rubbery strings called tendons.

1. Your brain sends signals to your muscles to do what you want.

Hey, a ball!

Kick the ball!

2. The muscles pull on the bones to move them into the right position.

Kick!

3. It all happens so fast, you don't need to think about what each muscle is doing.

This is happening all the time – whether you're walking along the street, keying in a text, chewing food or dancing to music. Even standing still without falling over uses lots of muscles! But exercise uses them more.

Muscle energy

To make you move, muscles have to contract, or shorten, so they can pull on your bones. To do this, they release energy inside their cells. This energy comes from the food you eat, especially meals that contain pasta, rice and bread.

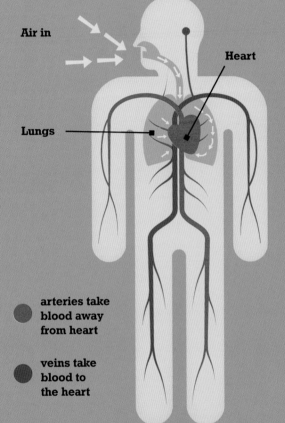

Air in

Heart

Lungs

arteries take blood away from heart

veins take blood to the heart

Pumping blood

To turn food into energy, your cells also need oxygen. When you breathe in, your lungs take oxygen out of the air and put it into your blood. Then your heart pumps the oxygen-filled blood all around your body inside your blood vessels. The blood delivers oxygen to every cell and returns to the heart and lungs.

Full power!

You've got enough energy in your muscles to give that ball a good kick. But when you carry on exercising for a long time – like playing a whole football game, or walking up a mountain – you need more energy. Your cells start turning stored food energy into extra energy, and for that they need extra oxygen.

1. So you start to breathe faster to get extra oxygen in...

2. ...and your heart starts beating faster to pump more oxygen to your cells.

3. All that extra blood pumping and muscles moving starts to warm you up – so you may start sweating to help you cool down.

But why is all this good for you? Turn the page to find out!

Why is exercise good for you?

Exercise can tire you out and even make your muscles feel sore. So why are we always being told to do it? Because exercise really is incredibly good for you and your body – in all kinds of ways.

What does exercise do for you?

Builds strength

When you exercise a lot, your body decides you need extra muscle power. So it builds more muscle, and you get stronger.

As your muscles pull on your bones, your bones get stronger too. Your body builds them up so they can cope with all that activity.

With stronger bones and muscles, you're less likely to break a bone, or develop problems like back pain – and it's easier to do everyday stuff, like running upstairs.

Improves circulation

Exercise makes your heart work hard, and pump blood around your body faster.

This makes your heart and blood vessels stronger, so you're less likely to get heart disease.

On top of that, all that extra blood flow helps other parts of your body too, such as your skin and hair roots. They get more oxygen, and other important things that your blood delivers, like vitamins and nutrients. So exercise can help with skin problems like acne, for example.

Gives you more energy

People often say exercise gives you extra energy. But exercise uses up energy – so how does that work?

Exercise speeds up your metabolism – the speed at which your body turns food and oxygen into energy. That means you start to feel more bouncy, wideawake and ready for action, even when you're not actually exercising.

Boosts your brain

Exercise also increases blood flow to your brain, and the extra oxygen helps your brain to work better. It can increase your concentration, and improve memory and problem-solving skills.

Makes you happier

Exercise makes your body release chemicals called endorphins, which make you feel happier and give you a 'glowing' feeling after you stop.

Exercise is also a brilliant way to reduce feelings of stress and anxiety. In fact, scientists have found it's one of the best ways to make people feel more positive about their lives and look forward to each new day.

Helps you sleep

After lots of exercise, your body will feel tired. That helps you fall asleep fast – instead of being kept awake by worries or feeling jittery. And getting enough sleep is really good for your health (see page 16).

What if you can't be bothered...?

Of course, if you're feeling upset or you aren't used to exercise, it can be hard to make yourself get up and move. This book contains lots of ideas for how to get started, build more exercise into your life or try new activities you might love.

Types of exercise

You might have heard people talking about the need to do different types of exercise. To get fit, you need to take exercise which improves stamina, strength and suppleness.

Constant cardio

Cardio is short for cardiovascular exercise, which means exercising your heart and lungs. It's exercise that you do continuously, like running. Your heart rate and breathing get faster, and you start to sweat.

Types of cardio exercise include:

| Running | Fast walking | Cycling | Swimming | Dance fitness classes, like Zumba |

Cardio exercise makes your heart and breathing muscles stronger, and improves your stamina, so you are able to exercise for longer without getting tired.

Short-burst strength

Strength-based exercise means working your muscles hard. You repeatedly use a set of muscles – by lifting a weight, for example. Then you take a rest and do it again.

Types of strength-based exercise include:

| Weightlifting | Push-ups | Pull-ups | Throwing a javelin |

Strength training makes the muscles you are working grow bigger and stronger. This increases your metabolism – how fast your body burns energy.

Mix them up!

Cardio exercise and strength exercise are both good for your body – and many types of exercise combine them, such as cycling, for example.

Cycling along is a cardio workout – it increases your breathing and heart rate.

Pushing down on the pedals to climb a hill is a strength workout for your legs.

It's also useful to improve your body's suppleness, which keeps it bending and moving easily. Dance, gymnastics and yoga are especially good for this.

.... but you also need loads of strength and suppleness to spring into the air for catching and scoring.

To play basketball, you need to run around for a long time...

That's why professional sportspeople do different types of exercise in their training.

Aerobic and anaerobic

Ever wondered what these words mean? Read on!

Aerobic = with oxygen

During most exercise, like dancing, your heart beats faster to pump enough blood to provide the oxygen your cells need, so you can keep going. That's aerobic (with oxygen) exercise.

But imagine you have to run very fast from a bull and scramble over a wall at high speed to escape.

Anaerobic = without oxygen

To get the extra boost your muscles need, your body will have to release stored energy anaerobically (without oxygen). This is a special way of releasing stored energy from your muscles, even when there isn't enough oxygen. Your muscles can do this, but only for a short time. Before long, it makes them really sore.

Pole vaulters and sprinters rely on short bursts of anaerobic energy.

What exercise can I do?

When people hear the word 'exercise', they might think of going to the gym and running on a treadmill, or joining a football team – which they might not want to do.

Everyone is different. You might not like sports, for example, because you don't like the pressure to win – but you love dancing with your mates. Or maybe you feel shy about dancing, but you'd make a great cross-country runner.

Everyone's body is different too. You may have a disability or illness that makes some activities difficult. But you could still find an exercise you enjoy. Take a look at these two pages to give you some ideas.

Dance
Humans are naturally inclined to dance to music.

At a party or festival
Dance classes
Zumba
Ballet
Street dance
Hip hop
Funk
Tap
Jazz dance
Cheerleading

Exercise
Exercise
Exercise

Gym
Gyms have loads of exercise equipment, activities and classes.

Rowing machine
Strength training
Spinning
Weightlifting
Yoga

Sports
There are dozens of sports clubs and teams you can join, in and out of school.

Football/Soccer
Hockey
Netball
Rugby
Cricket
Cross-country running
Rowing
Tennis
Badminton
Golf
Judo
Swimming
Basketball

Outdoors

Get fresh air and exercise at the same time!

Hiking
Camping
Geocaching
Orienteering
Climbing
Kayaking
Rollerblading
Horseriding
Sledging and snowman-building
Skiing
Trampolining
Cycling

Chores

Chores may not all be fun, but at least you know they're making you fitter!

Washing the car
Clearing up leaves or litter
Hanging up washing
Emptying bins
Sweeping or vacuuming

Exercise Exercise Exercise

Everyday exercise

You can also build exercise into daily life.

Take the stairs instead of the lift
Walk to the shops and carry a bag home
Help with the gardening
Cycle or walk to school
Play tag or hide-and-seek
Build sandcastles at the beach
Try a dance or exercise video game
Play or sing in a band

Don't stop moving!

Even when you can't do much exercise, just getting up and moving around is great for your body. If you have to do homework or stay in one place for a long time, you can break it up every so often by fetching a drink, having a stretch or going for a short walk or run.

Food and energy

We all need food to give us the energy to exercise – and even to move around at all. Body cells can only work if they get energy from food. So what do you need to eat to help you exercise?

Foods for energy

Your body mainly gets energy from foods called carbohydrates, or carbs.

Some carbs release energy slowly, so they keep you going for longer.

Some carbs turn into energy much faster. They can give you a quick energy boost, but it doesn't last long. So they are less useful for helping you exercise.

Wholemeal bread

Pasta

Porridge

Fruit juice

Sugar and sweets

Cakes and biscuits

Energy in, energy out

Energy is measured in units called calories. Most foods contain calories, but some have more than others.

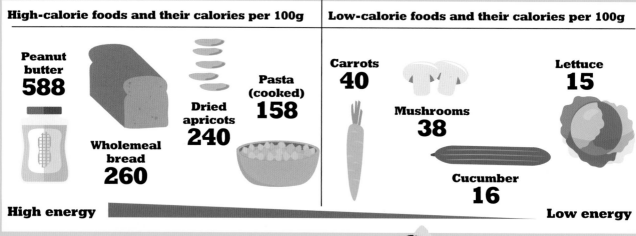

High-calorie foods and their calories per 100g	Low-calorie foods and their calories per 100g
Peanut butter **588**	Carrots **40**
Dried apricots **240**	Mushrooms **38**
Pasta (cooked) **158**	Lettuce **15**
Wholemeal bread **260**	Cucumber **16**

High energy ————————————————————— Low energy

You need to take in roughly the same amount of energy as you use up.

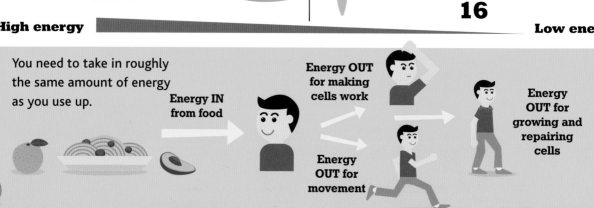

Energy IN from food

Energy OUT for making cells work

Energy OUT for movement

Energy OUT for growing and repairing cells

A balanced diet

If you do a lot of very active exercise, such as football, swimming, cycling or running, you'll probably find you get more hungry and need to eat more.

However, even if you are doing a lot of exercise, it's not ideal to just eat carbs. You need a wide range of foods to keep your body working well.

Protein

Protein builds muscle, repairs injuries and helps you grow bigger.

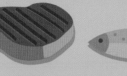

Meat   Fish   Cheese   Beans

Fats

Fats are vital to help your brain send signals around your body, and for quick reactions – vital in many sports!

Oils   Butter   Cheese   Nuts and seeds

Vitamins and minerals

Vitamins and minerals help many different parts of your body to work. Vitamin C, for example, found in fresh fruit and vegetables, helps your body to fight off germs. Minerals, such as calcium, are needed in tiny amounts to make your body work properly.

Fresh fruit and vegetables

Nuts and seeds

Milk and eggs contain calcium

Water

Your body is between 60 per cent and 70 per cent water. Body cells need to be filled with and surrounded by water to work properly. Your blood is mostly water too. You use water to flush out waste chemicals in your urine (wee), and it also comes out in breath and sweat.

So you need to replace all the water you lose – about two litres a day in total. Making sure there is enough water in your body is called being hydrated.

You can drink plain water or other drinks that are mostly water, like milk, tea or weak squash. If you're exercising a lot, or it's very hot, you'll sweat more, so you'll need more to drink.

Sleep

It's crazy to think that you will spend around a third of your life – that's one hour in every three, or about 27 years – crashed out, fast asleep. Yet if you didn't, you'd be very unhealthy indeed. Sleep is vital for keeping your body fit and healthy.

Scientists still aren't completely sure what sleep is for, or why we do so much of it. But they have found out a few important facts:

Sleep is essential for life. The longest anyone has been known to stay awake is about 11 days.

If you don't get the sleep you need, it can damage your concentration and decision-making powers, give you a headache or put you in an irritable, grouchy mood.

Sleep helps your body to repair injuries and fight germs. A lack of sleep can make you more likely to catch colds and flu, or have an acne breakout.

If you sleep well, you will move faster, have better co-ordination and get less tired when you're playing sport or doing other exercise. And if you get plenty of exercise, you'll sleep better too!

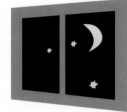

Dreams

Dreams may be linked to your brain's memory-sorting process, as they often feature a jumble of things that happened to you recently.

People often dream about things that are worrying them, too, like an upcoming test or moving house.

How much sleep?

Babies sleep a lot, but you need less and less sleep as you grow up.
People vary a bit in how much sleep they need, but on average, we sleep for...

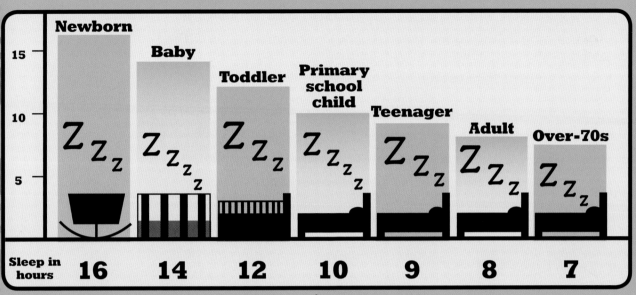

| Sleep in hours | 16 | 14 | 12 | 10 | 9 | 8 | 7 |

I can't sleep!

Insomnia, or being unable to sleep, is very common. It can help if you...

• Avoid looking at screens just before bed –
the bluish light can wake up your brain.

• Avoid coffee, alcohol or lots of food just before bed.
Instead, try drinking warm milk.

• Make sure your room is really dark at night.

• Write down any worries that are keeping you awake,
and leave them for the morning.

• Exercise during the day, to tire your body out.

Teenagers often go through a phase of pushing their bedtime later and later, and sleeping in later in the mornings. Some schools have tried starting later to allow for this. When they do, the students get more sleep, and produce better results.

Staying well

One thing that can seriously mess with your sport or dance classes, exercise or outdoor fun, is being ill. Flu, a nasty cold or food poisoning can make you feel terrible, and leave you stuck on the sofa, unable to leave the house. So how can you avoid illness?

Fighting fit

Exercise itself, and keeping physically fit, help your body to fight off germs.

The cells and chemicals that attack germs are carried in your blood. When you exercise, blood pumps around your body faster and more efficiently. This may help to kill germs faster, stopping them from invading and infecting you.

Exercise also reduces stress, and stress can make you more likely to get ill.

Invisible germs

Many illnesses, like colds and flu, mumps, measles, chicken pox, diarrhoea and earache, are caused by tiny, invisible germs. They can be single-celled bacteria, or even tinier viruses.

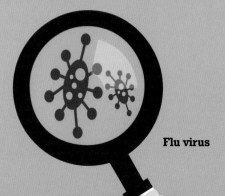

Flu virus

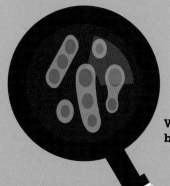

Whooping cough bacteria

Battling germs

Germs pass from person to person on unwashed hands, through the air in coughs and sneezes or in dirty water. Or they can be found in undercooked food or in soil, or be spread by insects.

To avoid, kill and generally outwit disease germs, you should...

- Always wash your hands after going to the toilet and before eating.

- Make sure fresh food is prepared and cooked properly, and kept chilled.

- Wash regularly, and avoid sharing things such as toothbrushes, towels and hairbrushes.

- Don't eat food that been sitting around all day at room temperature!

Flies can jump on it.

Germs can grow in it.

Asthma and exercise

Asthma is a condition that can make the tubes in your lungs tighten up, making it hard to breathe. It's very common – about 9 per cent of people are treated for asthma.

Unfortunately, exercise is one of the things that can trigger an asthma attack. These tips can help you avoid problems.

- Talk to your doctor about any new exercise you are planning to start.

- Always have your asthma treatment, such as an inhaler, with you when you exercise.

- Warm up slowly and do not push yourself too hard.

- Swimming is often great for people with asthma because the warm, damp air is good for their lungs.

19

Serious illnesses

In the western world, three serious diseases – cancer, cardiovascular disease and diabetes – are a very big problem. They cause more than half of all deaths. And physical activity, exercise and fitness are a big part of how we can beat them.

Cancer

Cancer is a type of disease in which body cells start to grow out of control. It can happen in many parts of the body, such as the skin, bowel, lungs or blood.

Some cancers can be cured, but it's still a big killer.

Cancer has many causes – but scientists have found that regular physical activity reduces the risk of some types of cancer, particularly breast, womb and bowel cancer.

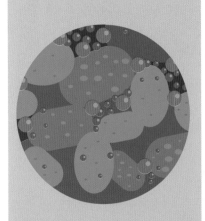

Cardiovascular disease

Cardiovascular disease means disease of the heart or blood vessels. It includes heart attacks and strokes – when the heart or brain is damaged by a clot in a blood vessel – and heart disease caused by blood vessels becoming blocked or narrowing.

These problems are much less common in people who take exercise, are a healthy weight and don't smoke.

Diabetes

Diabetes is a common disease that makes the levels of sugar in your blood rise too high. There are two types, Type 1 and Type 2.

Type 1 diabetes often begins early in life and it's not known what causes it.

Type 2 diabetes often strikes later in life. It's more common in people who exercise less and have an unhealthy diet or are overweight.

For both types of diabetes, exercise can help to control the illness.

Exercise and weight

Obesity – being very overweight – is becoming more common, and increases the risk of serious diseases like these.

When you exercise, you use up extra energy. This helps you to stay a healthy weight as you're more likely to use up spare energy from the food you eat.

However, exercise doesn't burn off a huge amount of extra calories. The main reason exercise is good for you is that it improves your blood flow, strength and overall health. To stay a healthy weight, you also need to eat healthily – ideally eating a wide range of foods, eating sensible portions and avoiding too much sugar (see page 14).

Smoking

There's also another massive risk factor for serious illness, and that's smoking. Avoiding smoking is one of the best things you can do for your health and fitness.

Smoking also makes your lungs work less well, so it can be harder to exercise if you're a smoker.

21

Get outdoors!

What would happen to you if you stayed indoors 24/7, and never went outside at all? You wouldn't be very well, that's what. Although too much sunshine can be harmful, it's actually very important to get some time in the sun.

Sunlight and vitamin D

We get most of our essential vitamins from our food. But one vitamin, vitamin D, is also made in our skin when sun shines on it. It can be difficult to get enough of it from food alone.

Vitamin D is important because it...

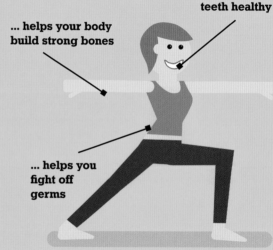

... helps your body build strong bones

... helps keep your teeth healthy

... helps you fight off germs

Rickets

A shortage of vitamin D can lead to a disease called rickets, in which your bones become soft and weak. In the past, rickets was more common, and sometimes caused children to grow up with bent leg bones.

Scientists think getting plenty of sunlight may also reduce the risk of some other diseases, such as TB (tuberculosis) and MS (multiple sclerosis).

What about skin cancer?

You're probably more aware of the dangers of the sun, than its benefits. Getting sunburnt is very bad for your skin, and can increase the risk of skin cancer – which is why you are told to...

- Wear suncream ☑
- Wear a hat ☑
- Keep covered up ☑

... in strong sunshine.

So it is good to take care in the sun, but not to avoid it altogether.

Get some fresh air!

People often talk about fresh air being good for you, but is it really? Yes!

- Humans breathe in oxygen, and breathe out a waste gas, carbon dioxide. If you're indoors for a long time, the levels of oxygen in the air will reduce. Getting outside gives you fresher, oxygen-rich air.

- The air in cities can be polluted with gases and particles from vehicle engines and factories. Getting away to the countryside or seaside gives your body a break from the polluted air.

- Whether you are outdoors in the countryside or in your local park, you'll also improve your health by absorbing vitamin D from sunlight. Scientists have also discovered that people's mood improves if they spend time outdoors in natural environments.

Don't overdo it!

So exercise, getting outdoors, moving around and being active are definitely good for you. But is it possible to exercise too much, or too hard?

The answer is yes. Too much of anything can be harmful, and exercise is no exception.

Start slowly

If you're not used to exercise, or haven't done any at all for a while, it's not a great idea to suddenly try to run a marathon or lift a huge weight!

Your body probably won't be strong enough, so something like that could cause an injury. Instead, it's best to start gradually and slowly.

If you have asthma or any other health conditions, or you've recently recovered from a serious illness, it's a good idea to talk to your doctor about any new exercise you plan to start.

• Buy some sports trainers and gradually increase the distance that you run. Your local running club may have a youth section.

• Try a dance or yoga class, where the instructor can help you get started.

• Join a sports or martial arts club, where you work through a series of levels.

It shouldn't hurt!

Exercise should NOT be horribly painful. Ignore phrases like 'No pain, no gain!'

If it hurts, that's your body's way of telling you to stop. You might need to see a doctor if you're worried that exercise is causing you a lot of pain, or that you might have an injury.

Lifting heavy weights can cause muscle strains.

People sometimes get injured during impact sports such as rugby.

Some sports, including horseriding, can be dangerous if you don't have the right equipment and knowledge. They should always be done with an instructor.

Top-level sportspeople may suffer pain, but that's because they're pushing their bodies to the limit. You don't have to!

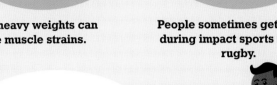

Exercise addiction

People can sometimes get addicted to exercise, and the feeling of achievement or the endorphin 'glow' it can give you. Sometimes, they may feel that exercise will help them get a 'perfect' body, and feel scared of not exercising enough.

If this happens, you can end up exercising so much, that it starts to wear you out. You might also miss out on things like social occasions or schoolwork. You could end up feeling really stressed – which isn't the point of exercise at all! Rest, relaxation and downtime are also important – for your body, and for your happiness too.

If this could be happening to you or someone you know, it's a good idea to talk to a doctor, or a teacher or parent you trust, as they should be able to help.

Fit for the future

Exercise, activity and fitness can help you have a healthy life for the whole of your life – if you keep at it! But staying active through all the stages of your life can be a challenge.

If exercise is something you can build into everyday life, and do with friends or for fun, it will become a lifelong habit.

If it's a chore, or something you have to fit in between all the other things in your busy life, it's much harder to keep it up.

Enjoy it!

It's much easier to do exercise you enjoy. Find the activities you really like and feel passionate about – whether that's a team sport, tap dancing, diving, running, Taekwondo or synchronised swimming – it doesn't matter, as long as you love it.

You don't have to do exercise that isn't right for you, even if it is the latest fashion and everyone else loves it. Many people find yoga calming and relaxing, for example – but if you find it uncomfortable or too hard, it's OK to look for something else!

Healthy options

You can also get everyday exercise by choosing to do things in ways that get you moving and use up energy. If you can, walk instead of taking the car or bus, take stairs instead of lifts, try active hobbies like drama or walk a dog!

Find like minds

Exercise can be more fun, and easier to make time for if it's part of your social life too. Look out for friends who you can do your favourite exercise with, and you'll always look forward to it.

A running group

Camping and hiking with other families

Going dancing with your mates

Every bit helps

There will be times in your life when exercise is the last thing on your mind – like when you've just had a baby, or have an illness or injury.

But that's not a disaster. Any kind of moving around is better than none, even if it's a short stroll or a few household jobs. When you're ready to start doing more, you can gradually add new activities or classes.

An active career

If you're an especially sporty, active or strong person, you could end up doing something related to sport or exercise as your job. You could even represent your country at your chosen sport!

Personal trainer

There are also many other careers where being fit and active, or working outdoors, are a big part of the job:

Soldier

Firefighter

Police officer

Builder

Zookeeper

Exercise options

These lists may give you ideas about sports, activities or fitness classes to try.

Dance and dance fitness classes

Jazz dance
Tap dance
Ballet
Ballroom dancing
Street dance
Hip-hop
Modern dance
Bollywood dance
Belly dancing
Folk or country dancing
Cheerleading
Salsa
Zumba
Bokwa
Batuka
Sh'bam

Sports

Football/soccer
Five-a-side
Rugby
Cricket
Hockey
Lacrosse
Ice hockey
Athletics
Netball
Basketball
Volleyball
Baseball
Handball
Tennis
Badminton
Squash
Table tennis
Running
Cycling
Swimming
Synchronised swimming
Ice skating
Archery
Golf
Gymnastics
Roller derby

Martial arts

Judo
Karate
Aikido
Jujitsu
Boxing
Taekwondo
Kickboxing
Capoeira
T'ai chi
Wrestling
Fencing

Outdoor activities

Hiking
Camping
Kayaking
Climbing
Cycling
Hillrunning
Orienteering
Geocaching
Jogging
Rollerblading
Skateboarding
Wheelchair motocross
BMX/stunt biking
Skiing
Snowboarding
Horseriding
Trampolining
Doing zip lines
Surfing
Snorkelling
Paddleboarding

Gym classes and activities

Weightlifting
Kettlebells
Running machine
Rowing machine
Cross-trainer
Boxercise
Bodypump
Circuit training
Spinning
Step
Yoga
Pilates

Everyday activities

Vacuuming
Window cleaning
Tidying
Grocery shopping
Changing beds
Hanging out washing
Car cleaning
Gardening
Taking the stairs
Walking
Dog walking
Dancing to music
Fitness video games

Glossary

aerobic Exercise that uses a supply of oxygen from the lungs to make muscles work.

anaerobic Exercise in which muscles are forced to work for a while without a supply of oxygen.

asthma Illness in which tubes in the lungs become narrower, making it hard to breathe.

blood clot A lump of thickened blood.

blood vessels The tubes (arteries, veins and capillaries) that carry blood around the body.

calories Units used to measure the amount of energy contained in food.

cancer Disease in which some of the body's cells grow out of control.

carbohydrates (carbs) A type of food nutrient that gives the body energy.

carbon dioxide A gas that is breathed out by animals and taken in by plants.

cardio (cardiovascular) Exercise that speeds up your heartbeat and makes your heart and blood vessels healthier.

cardiovascular disease Disease of the heart or blood vessels.

circulation The way blood flows around and around inside your body.

dehydration Not having enough water in your body.

diabetes An illness that makes it hard for the body to control the amount of sugar in the blood.

endorphins Chemicals released by the brain, often during exercise, which make you feel good.

fat A type of nutrient that helps protect the body and helps brain cells to work.

food poisoning Various types of illness caused by germs eaten in food that has not been properly cooked or stored, or has gone off.

geocaching an activity when an item, or a container holding a number of items, is hidden somewhere for GPS users to find using instructions posted on the Internet.

germs Tiny living things that can cause some types of diseases.

heart attack Sudden damage to the heart because of loss of blood supply, caused by a blood clot or blocked blood vessel.

hydration Getting enough water into your body.

insomnia Being unable to sleep.

mental health The health of your mind and emotions.

metabolism The rate at which your body works and turns food into energy.

minerals Natural, non-living substances such as iron and calcium that are found in foods and are essential for the body in small amounts.

musculoskeletal system The set of bones and muscles in your body that work together to make you move.

nutrients The chemicals found in food that give your body what it needs to function.

oxygen A gas found in the air, which humans and other animals need in order to live.

protein A type of nutrient that helps the body to grow new cells and repair damage.

stamina Being able to carry on exercising for long periods of time.

stress Mental or emotional tension or exhaustion.

stroke Damage to the brain caused by a blood clot or leak in a blood vessel.

suppleness Being able to bend and move the body smoothly.

tendons Rubbery strings that connect the ends of muscles to bones.

vitamins Chemicals that are essential for the body and which are found in some foods.

Further information

Health and fitness books

303 Kid-Approved Exercises and Active Games
by Kimberly Wechsler, 2013

Breathe: Yoga for Teens
by Mary Kaye Chryssicas, 2007

The Ultimate Book of Martial Arts
by Fay Goodman, 2015

Children's Book of Sport
Published by Dorling Kindersley, 2011

101 Things to Do Outside
Published by Weldon Owen, 2016

Websites

TeensHealth: Why Exercise is Wise
kidshealth.org/en/teens/exercise-wise.html

Explore the 'This Girl Can' website and get inspired to become more active
www.thisgirlcan.co.uk/

SafeTeens: Exercise and Fitness
www.safeteens.org/nutrition-exercise/exercise-fitness/

CYH Teen Health: Exercise
www.cyh.com/HealthTopics/HealthTopicDetails.aspx?p=243&np=292&id=2393

Note to parents and teachers: Every effort has been made by the Publishers to ensure that these websites are suitable for children, that they are of the highest educational value, and that they contain no inappropriate or offensive material. However, because of the nature of the Internet, it is impossible to guarantee that the contents of these sites will not be altered. We strongly advise that Internet access is supervised by a responsible adult.

Index